BIG AND BEASTLY
DINOSAURS

The words and pictures of
Big and Beastly Dinosaurs are
original and have been specially
commissioned for Tesco.

Published by
Tesco Stores Limited
Created by Brilliant Books Ltd
84–86 Regent Street
London W1B 5RR

First published 2000
ISBN 1-84221-124-2

Text and Illustrations © 2000 Brilliant Books Ltd
Printed by Printer Trento S.r.l., Italy
Reproduction by Colourpath, England

1 3 5 7 9 10 8 6 4 2

fun to learn
collection

BIG AND BEASTLY
DINOSAURS

**Written by
Sue Conway**

**Illustrated by
Karl Richardson**

Ankylosaurus

Ankylosaurus was one of the biggest dinosaurs around. It was so big that it wasn't frightened of being attacked by vicious meat eaters.

Ankylosaurus was as big as a tank and weighed as much as 100 people!

It was a vegetarian, and liked to eat leaves, moss and twigs.

Unfortunately, it was also a real dimwit with a very thick skull and a very little brain.

The top side of its body was covered in spines and bony scales.

It had a very long tail with a big club of bone on the end – which it used to thump its enemies.

Tyrannosaurus

The most vicious of all the dinosaurs, it was
the one all the other dinosaurs
really wanted to avoid!

Its mouth was so big,
it could gobble up
a human in one gulp.

It was tall enough to
peer over the top of a
double-decker bus.

Each one of
Tyrannosaurus's
teeth was as long
as a banana.

Its name means tyrant lizard.

Tyrannosaurus's breath would have smelled terrible – it stank of decaying flesh!

A grown man would only reach up to the knee of a Tyrannosaurus.

Triceratops

With a huge crest of solid bone and three scary horns above its nose and eyes, Triceratops was very well protected.

Triceratops lived in groups to help protect themselves from attack by vicious meat-eating dinosaurs like Tyrannosaurus.

Triceratops means three-horned face.

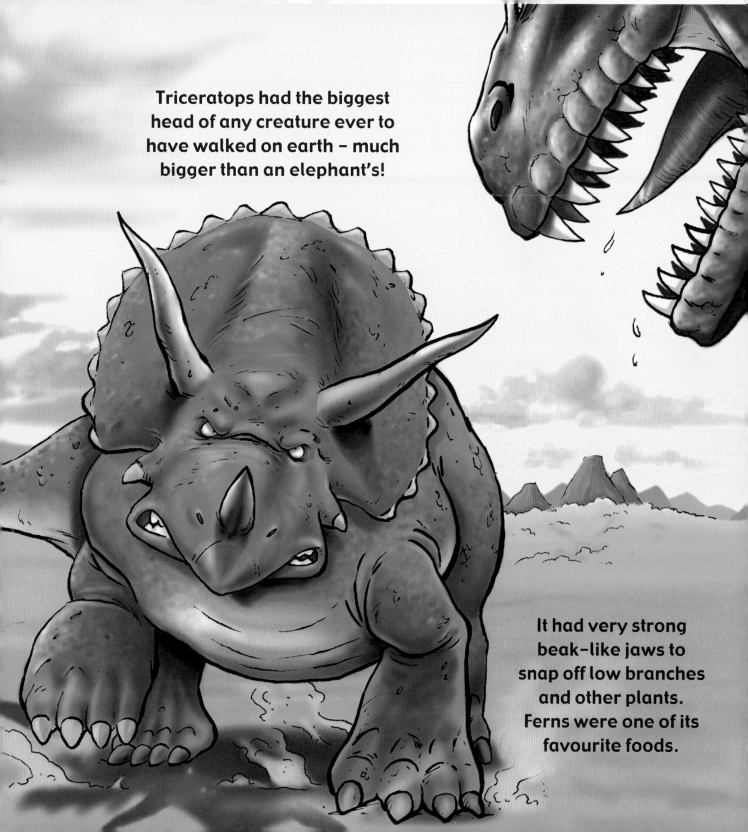

Triceratops had the biggest head of any creature ever to have walked on earth – much bigger than an elephant's!

It had very strong beak-like jaws to snap off low branches and other plants. Ferns were one of its favourite foods.

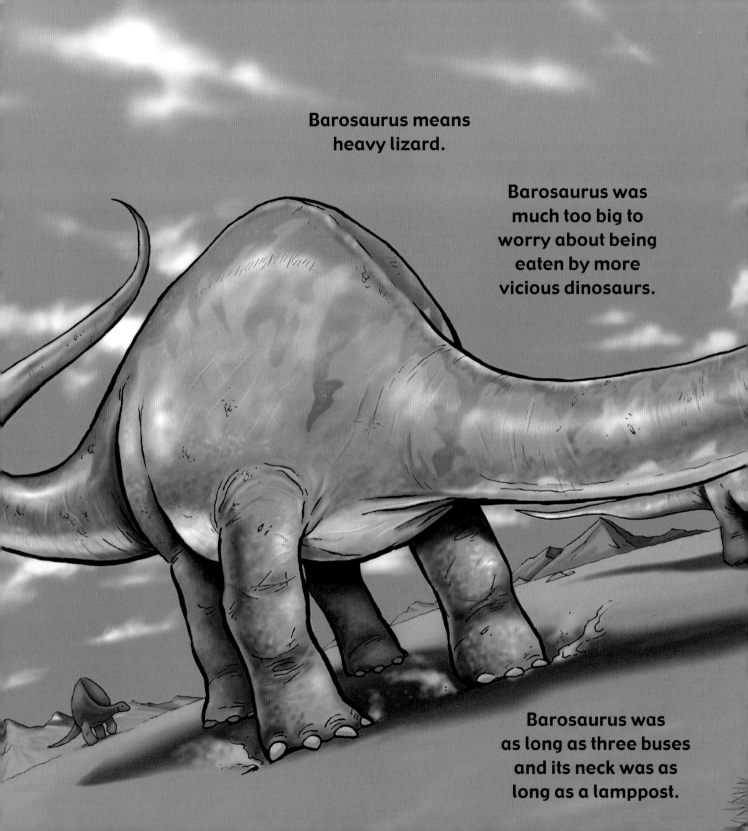

Barosaurus means
heavy lizard.

Barosaurus was
much too big to
worry about being
eaten by more
vicious dinosaurs.

Barosaurus was
as long as three buses
and its neck was as
long as a lamppost.

Barosaurus

Enormous Barosaurus was so big and so stupid,
it could have sat on an elephant and
not even noticed!

Luckily for smaller
dinosaurs, it was
a vegetarian and ate
ferns and leaves from
very tall trees.

Barosaurus's neck was
so long, it couldn't hold
its head up for too long
without getting dizzy!

Brachiosaurus was as long as a tennis court.

Brachiosaurus made use of its long neck to nibble leaves and cones at the top of very tall trees.

Brachiosaurus

Brachiosaurus is one of the tallest animals
ever to have walked on earth.

It weighed as much
as 12 elephants and
each of its steps made
the ground shake!

Brachiosaurus
was taller than
a three-storey
building.

It couldn't walk very
fast and a human
could have caught up
with it quite easily.

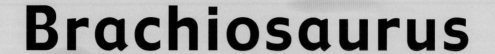

Diplodocus

One of the longest of all dinosaurs, Diplodocus was longer than a swimming-pool. Despite its enormous body, it had a teeny-weeny brain!

Its legs alone were the height of lampposts. And it needed its long neck to reach back down to the ground for food.

It was probably a bit of a klutz... Oops! There goes another tree!

Diplodocus had to eat non-stop, to supply its enormous body with enough food.

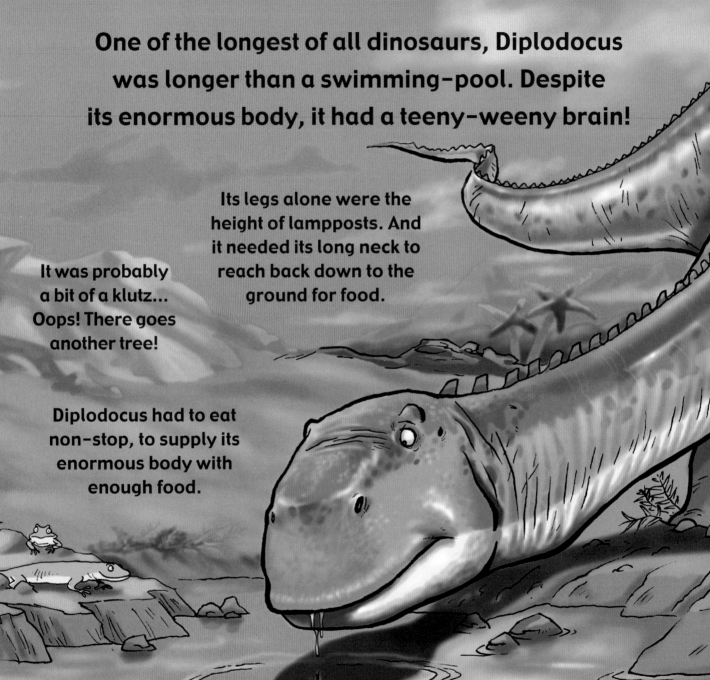

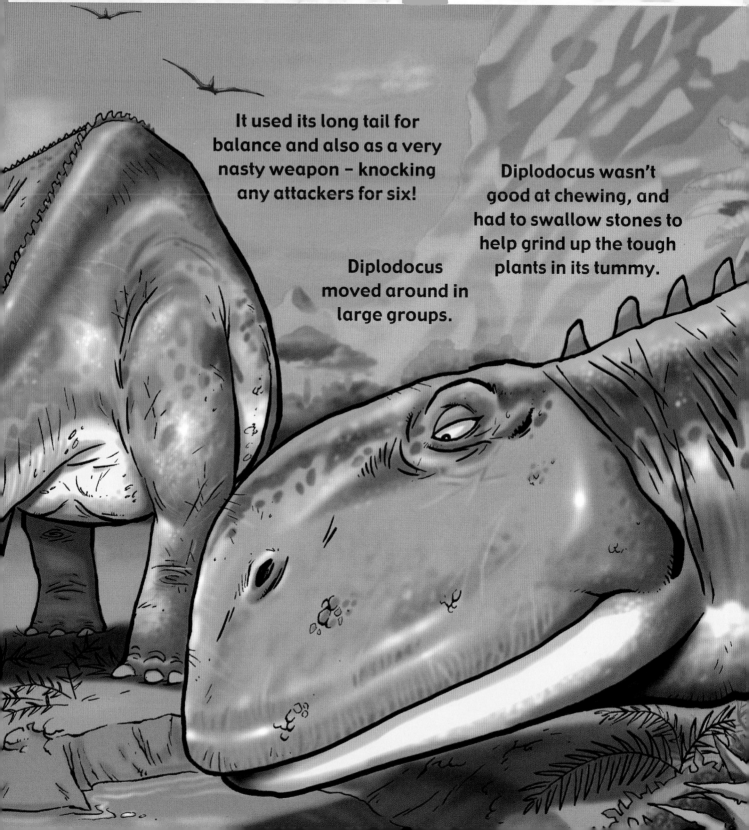

Iguanadon could walk on all fours, or just on its hind legs – when it wanted to reach something high up, or run away from an attacker!

Iguanadon means iguana tooth – an iguana is a type of big lizard, alive today, which lives in hot countries and eats insects.

Iguanadon

Iguanadon was as tall as a giraffe but four times as long.

Iguanadon ate plants. Unlike most dinosaurs, it was a natural-born chewer, so its food was already pulped before it even swallowed.

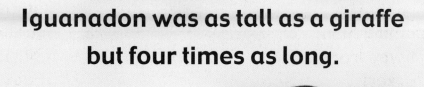

Iguanadon had huge spikes on its thumbs that it used as weapons in a fight. But poor old Iguanadon wouldn't have stood much chance if it was caught by a Tyrannosaurus.

Pachycephalosaurus

Pachycephalosaurus was a bit of a toughy, fighting – head on – with other members of its group, in the way that deer do today.

Pachycephalosaurus means thick–headed reptile.

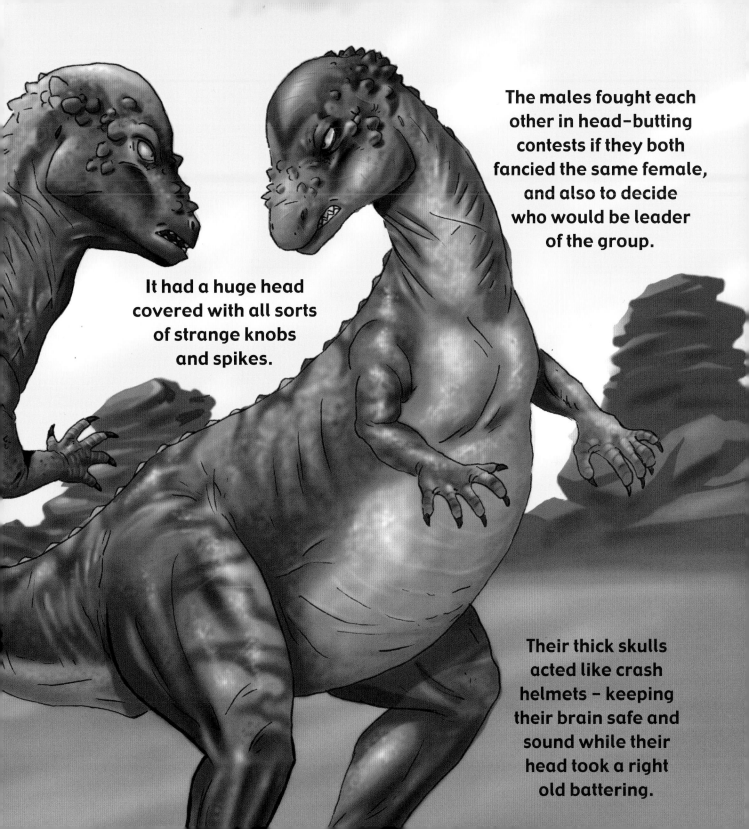

The males fought each other in head-butting contests if they both fancied the same female, and also to decide who would be leader of the group.

It had a huge head covered with all sorts of strange knobs and spikes.

Their thick skulls acted like crash helmets - keeping their brain safe and sound while their head took a right old battering.

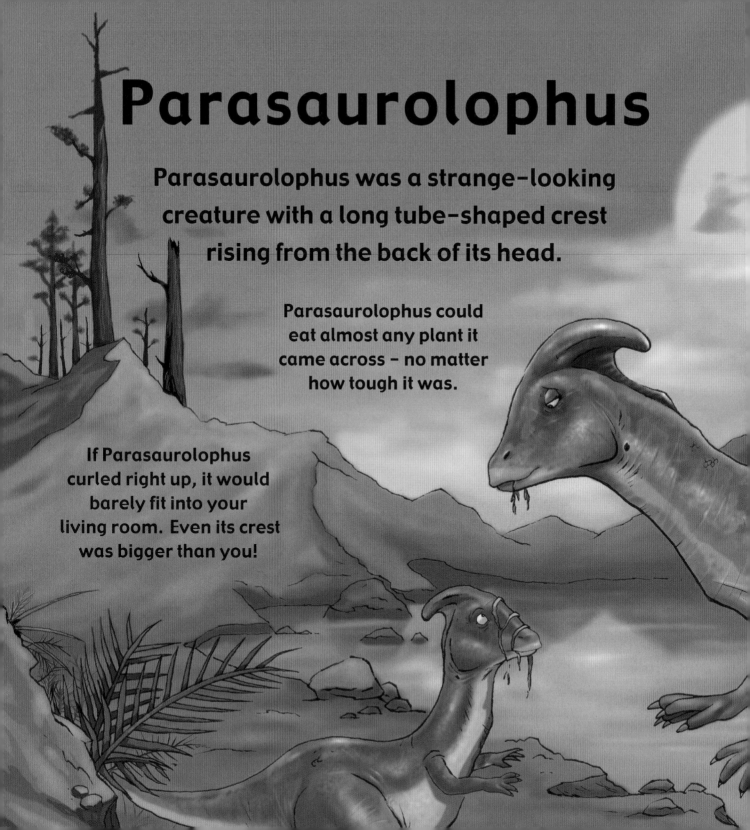

Parasaurolophus

Parasaurolophus was a strange-looking creature with a long tube-shaped crest rising from the back of its head.

Parasaurolophus could eat almost any plant it came across – no matter how tough it was.

If Parasaurolophus curled right up, it would barely fit into your living room. Even its crest was bigger than you!

Its crest may have been used to attract a mate or scare off an enemy. It was hollow and if it blew through it, it could have made a number of different honking and squawking sounds to warn its friends of danger.

It had a bill like a duck and up to 2000 teeth arranged in tight rows in its mouth.

Stegosaurus

Stegosaurus is easy to recognise by the double row of plates running down its back.

Stegosaurus means roofed lizard, because the bony plates on its back look a bit like the top of a roof.

It was as big as a large lorry, with back legs as tall as a long ladder.

Despite its size, Stegosaurus had a brain the size of a walnut!

It had very weak teeth and could only eat soft plants.

When it was angry, the plates along its back may have gone a scary shade of red.

Its only real weapons were four nasty spikes on the end of its tail, which could do a lot of damage when it lashed out with it in a fight.

Compsognathus

Tiny Compsognathus was no bigger than a hen and was one of the smallest known dinosaurs.

Anyone fancy a snack?

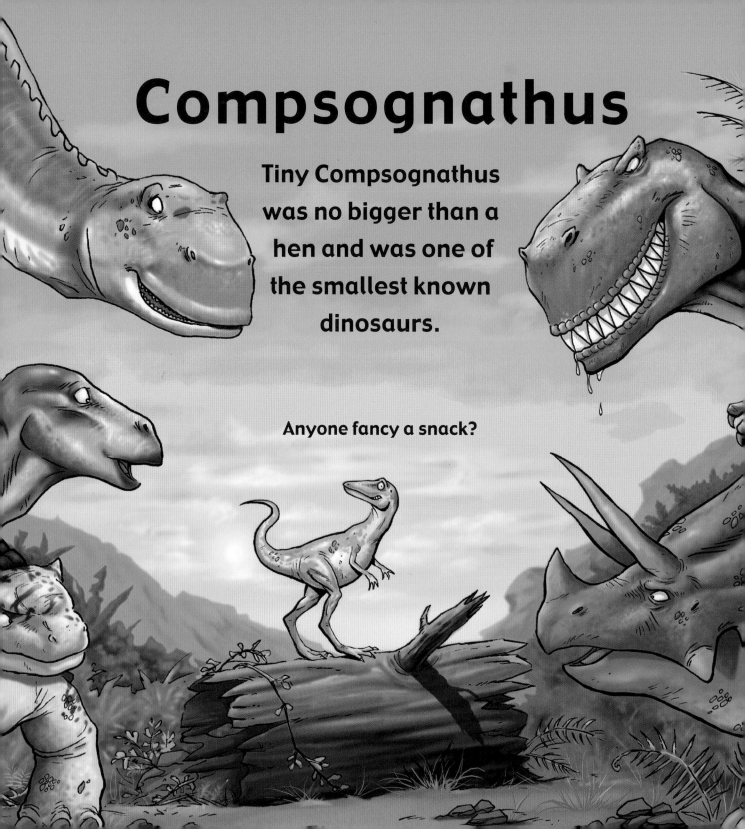